A souvenir guide

Wordsworth House and Garden

Cockermouth, The Lakes

National Trust

A Poet's Birthplace

Wordsworth House is the birthplace and childhood home of world-famous romantic poet William and his sister and lifelong companion Dorothy, and it was here that he learned the twin loves of nature and literature that were to shape both their lives.

Tragic loss

This happy life ended in March 1778, when Ann died, aged just 31, at her parents' home in Penrith. She had left the children there to go to London and returned in poor health. The family attributed her death to sleeping in damp sheets, but pneumonia or consumption is a more likely cause.

William, who later described his mother as the 'heart and hinge of all our learnings and our loves', was not quite eight. He wrote that their father 'never recovered his usual cheerfulness of mind'.

Dorothy, William's closest playmate, was sent to live with Ann's cousin in Halifax, and Richard and William became pupils at Hawkshead Grammar School, returning home only in the holidays. It would be nine years before William and Dorothy met again.

In December 1783, the children lost their father too. John had been called to Millom, 40 miles to the south, in his role as local coroner. He got lost riding home and spent the night on the fells, catching a severe chill. He never recovered and died in his bed. The house was emptied, the keys handed back and the Wordsworth children left for ever, to be cared for by relatives.

Above **Profile portrait of Dorothy Wordsworth**

Left **Portrait of William Wordsworth by William Hancock, 1798**

Opposite **The young William and Dorothy loved to play in the garden of Wordsworth House**

Below **The children's bedroom**

In 1765, aged just 24, lawyer John Wordsworth moved into what is now called Wordsworth House. It was a very grand 'tied' house, which came rent-free with his job as agent for the Cumberland estates of Sir James Lowther, one of England's richest men.

The following year, John married Ann Cookson, the 19-year-old daughter of a prosperous Penrith draper. It must have been quite daunting for her to leave her home above the shop to become mistress of such a splendid house.

Happy childhood

John and Ann had five children: Richard in 1768, William in 1770, Dorothy in 1771, John in 1772 and Christopher in 1774. In poems such as *The Prelude*, William recalls his childhood in Cockermouth with great warmth.

During the 18th century, theorists such as Locke and Rousseau advised parents that children should be allowed to behave naturally and play in the open air, rather than being cosseted and restricted as in previous centuries. John and Ann seem to have adopted this approach, and William loved to be outdoors. He also enjoyed reading his father's 'golden store' of books.

A Changing House

Today, Wordsworth House is decorated and furnished as it might have been when William and his family lived here in the 1770s. However, it has had many other occupants.

Despite an inscription over the back door claiming it was built by Joshua Lucock, High Sheriff of Cumberland, in 1745, the house was constructed sometime between 1670 and 1690 and belonged, in the early years, to a man named William Bird. Designed to impress, its grand scale would have had quite an impact on Cockermouth's other residents, whose homes were far more modest.

Fashion statement

The first major changes are thought to have been made in 1744, when Lucock bought it – and a pew in the local church – for £350. The county's senior judicial figure, he wanted his home to reflect his considerable standing.

It is believed he was responsible for adding the fashionable sash windows and the porch, and internal woodwork and plasterwork in a rich classical style.

By the 1760s, the house was owned by John Wordsworth's employer, Sir James Lowther. John is thought to have made only minor decorative changes in the early years of his tenancy, but there is evidence that in about 1780 he updated the fireplaces with elegantly carved overmantels.

After John's death the house was tenanted by lawyers representing the Lowthers' interests. In 1885, it was bought by local auctioneer Robinson Mitchell. By the 1930s, Wordsworth House was home to the Ellis family.

A coat of limewash

The front of the house is rendered in lime and finished in terracotta-coloured limewash. The streaks caused by the run off from the stone sills are a natural feature and would have been present in the 18th century, when frequent repainting was not practical.

Evidence for the colour, which was reapplied in 1985, was found under the eaves – the house had previously been white for some years. Local paper *The Times & Star* complained the change 'does little to enhance the appearance of the building'.

First impressions

The front garden is laid out as it might have been in the 1770s, based on an archaeological study carried out in 2004. It is a courtyard garden typical of the age, designed to show the status of the owner and make a good impression on visitors and passers-by.

Two circular flower-beds are surrounded by sandstone flags and there are clipped box balls on either side of the gate. The formal effect is softened by herbs and perennials including roses, foxgloves, poppies, geraniums and irises.

Left The house before it was re-limewashed

Below left Odille Ellis on the front steps

Below right Odille's brother Billy by the front rockery

Opposite The house front and garden

A Family Home

For 30 years from 1907, Wordsworth House was home and surgery to a succession of GPs. From 1931–37, Dr Edward Ellis lived here with his family. His daughter Odille, who was five when they moved in, later shared some dramatic memories.

Odille's recollections included several occasions when Wordsworth House could have burnt down. She once set her bedroom curtains alight by wrapping them round a gas mantle, while in the grand drawing room more than one cotton wool-decked Christmas tree went up in flames thanks to the real candles.

Fish and chips

She also recalled the family eating fish and chips out of newspaper at a small table in the drawing room (illustrated on page 16). She slept in the room we present as Ann's bedroom. The neighbouring 'closet' was

Above Adelaide Goodlad (left) was involved in the 1937 campaign to save the house. Her daughter Elizabeth (right) has worked as a housekeeping assistant at Wordsworth House for over ten years

The brink of disaster

In 1937, Dr Ellis sold Wordsworth House to Cumberland Motor Services so the company could demolish it and build a bus station. When the plan became public, townspeople formed a committee and, with the help of donations from around the world, raised £1,625 to buy it.

The house was handed over to the National Trust in 1938 and had its official public opening on 3 June 1939. It was tenanted, with only limited visitor access, until 1979, when it was opened more fully. In 2004, more than £1 million was invested to return Wordsworth House to what it would have been in William and Dorothy's time: a bustling Georgian family home.

Good as new

Today, the formal rooms (at the front of the house) are furnished with antiques from the 18th century. You are welcome to sit on the window seats, but please don't touch anything else. Replica furnishings for the informal 'hands-on' rooms (at the back) were made by specialist craftspeople and conservators. Please make yourself at home in these rooms – and get a real feel for how the 'middling sort' lived in the 1770s.

her toy cupboard, and the store room by the stairs was the family's bathroom.

Odille's parents' room, now shown as the children's bedroom, was connected to the back door of the surgery (beside the current reception area's garden entrance) by a speaking tube, so anyone who needed the doctor during the night could summon him.

In pre-NHS days, many people settled their bills in kind. A local artist exchanged pictures for treatment, while a farmer paid with a pony, which was put temporarily in the back garden. Odille remembered: 'Father sat me on it and went to take a photograph. The pony moved off, I fell off and it finished up breaking his cold frames.'

She used to earn sweets by ferrying medicines to the bus stance so the drivers could deliver them to neighbouring villages.

Left Odille and her mother in the greenhouse, which was in the small walled garden

Life with the Wordsworths

The Wordsworths were a family of the 'middling sort' living in a grand and spacious house. Relative to most other people in Cockermouth at the time, theirs was a very comfortable existence.

Ann Wordsworth would have overseen the running of the household. She probably relied on popular household manuals such as Martha Bradley's *The British Housewife* and *The Servant's Directory* by Hannah Glasse, which provided encyclopaedic instruction in successful housekeeping.

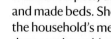

The Wordsworths employed a modest, but standard, range of servants, including a maid-of-all-work, a manservant, an occasional nursemaid for the children, and a jobbing gardener.

A maid's work

The lot of the maid-of-all-work was by far the hardest. Records show one girl, Amy, worked for the family for several years. Starting before anyone else was up, she would have cleaned and laid fires, emptied chamberpots, washed floors, brushed carpets, dusted and tidied, and aired and made beds. She would also have prepared the household's meals and spent at least one day a week washing their clothes.

For this, she earned £4 a year – at a time when John paid his clerk £20 and he himself received £100 and use of this house from Sir James Lowther. Amy was paid in six-monthly instalments, which tells us she lived in – if she had lived out, she would have been given her money weekly to pay for food and rent.

Life in livery

The manservant, who earned £4 4 shillings and also lived in, had far less to do. Despite this, John's accounts show he had difficulty filling the position, with payments to a succession of troublesome individuals, one of whom appears to have robbed him. One man, Bill Nelson, was employed for two separate periods.

The manservant was trusted with jobs requiring more skill, such as cleaning silver and glassware. It is likely that he was also responsible for the candles which lit the house. Tallow candles (made from rendered animal fat) would have been used most frequently. Wax ones, which were expensive, were kept for special occasions.

The manservant may also have cleaned the stables – where the house's reception area is now – and looked after his master's horses. In the afternoon, he would have changed into a smart livery coat to act as the household's footman, answering the front door and waiting on John and his guests.

Although the maid and manservant lived in, they wouldn't have had rooms of their own. The maid might have slept on a pull-out bed in the children's room or in the small room next door which, by the 1930s, had become the bathroom, while the manservant could have slept by the kitchen fire or in the hayloft above the stables – where the café is today.

Opposite left An 18th-century kitchen, illustrated in Robert Smith's *The Compleat English Cook* (1725)

Opposite right Costumed servants making a bed

Left It was the manservant's duty to make sure the clocks were wound

A Living, Working Home

John Wordsworth's accounts show he was extremely busy and often away from home. He rode long distances around Sir James's Cumberland estates, holding manor courts to arbitrate on local disputes, inspecting properties and collecting rents.

John also defended Sir James in legal matters and canvassed support for him at election time, all of which earned him a salary of £100 a year. In addition, he ran a lucrative private legal practice.

The entrance hall ✎

With its fluted columns and imposing staircase, the hall was designed to impress. However, only the most important guests would have entered here – most people would have used the back door. Clients waiting to see John might have sat in the hall. The bench, made of Cumbrian oak, is a copy of an 18th-century original.

The front office ✎

One of the smartest rooms in the house, with fine panelling and an elaborate cornice, this may well have been John's office. His mahogany desk may have been made for this room. It is dated 1766 – the year he and Ann married. On it are copies of some of the letters and other documents he wrote here.

After John died, a notice in *The Cumberland Pacquet* advertised the sale of his belongings, including 'a great Variety of valuable Prints, glassed and framed'. The prints on the walls are of the type he is likely to have owned.

Right John's desk in the front office

The Tyrant of the North

Sir James Lowther (1736–1802) was one of the most powerful men in England. He inherited a massive fortune and vast estates, including the Whitehaven collieries, at the age of 14. In 1761, he married Lady Mary Stuart, whose father became Prime Minister the following year.

Sir James's ambition was to control all ten parliamentary seats in Cumberland and Westmorland. He spent £58,060 acquiring a majority of Cockermouth's 278 burgage plots, whose owners could nominate the town's two MPs without an election. His ruthlessness earned him the nickname 'the Tyrant of the North'.

On either side of the desk are mezzotints of King George III and Queen Charlotte. There are also 18th-century maps of Cumberland and Westmorland, including, on the right of the fireplace, one dedicated to Sir James.

The back office ✎

This simple room may have housed John's clerk, who would have worked long hours keeping records, copying documents and receiving tenants. One man, William Arnott, stayed for ten years, earning £5 a quarter.

The elm desk and stool and pine plan chest are based on contemporary examples. Among the scattered papers are items likely to have been used by a clerk, including a wax-jack (a self-snuffing candle), ink pot and quills. Estate maps on the walls include a reproduction of Thomas Donald's 1774 map of Cumberland.

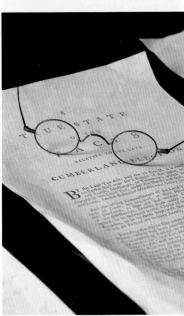

Above left **The clerk at work**

Left **Documents on John's desk**

A place to
entertain

The dining room ✎

The dining room would have been one of the Wordsworths' best rooms, probably used only for dinner parties and special family occasions. As a prominent figure in Cockermouth, John may have played host to friends and business associates, and Ann would have been anxious to provide an impressive display of food and drink.

Dinner parties

The Wordsworths' guests would have sat down in late afternoon and may have carried on eating and drinking for several hours, the women at one end of the table, the men at the other.

In sophisticated London circles, an arrangement known as 'promiscuous dining' – where men and women alternated around the table – was coming into fashion, but this took longer to catch on in the provincial north.

The paintings

The view of Cockermouth by Samuel Crosthwaite above the fireplace (illustrated on page 21) dates from around 1860, but the vista would have been recognisable to the Wordsworths.

The portraits are of brothers-in-law Isaac Littledale (left) and Thomas Hartley, who both lived in Whitehaven. Isaac was a merchant, Thomas a ship owner and co-founder of Hartley's Bank.

Isaac's daughter married the son of John's brother Richard, Whitehaven's Collector of Customs, so they would have moved in the same social circle as John and Ann, and may have dined in this room.

The table is set as it might have been for a small party – the dishes might have included roast meats, pies, vegetables in butter sauce and a selection of sweets.

Depending on what they were eating, diners would have conveyed it to their mouths on sharp two-pronged forks, wide-bladed knives or spoons.

To save them having to stagger elsewhere to relieve themselves, a chamberpot was kept in the sideboard. After the meal, the women would go up to the drawing room to drink tea, while the men stayed here, drinking toasts and possibly getting very drunk.

Status symbols

The only room with decorative plasterwork on the ceiling, this reflects its high status. Paint analysis shows most of the decoration dates from 1744–6. The fire surround was updated at the same time, although John may have added the late 18th-century decorative overmantel.

The furniture, such as the Hepplewhite chairs, is typical of a middle-class Georgian dining room, as is the mid-green paint colour. There are no curtains, because soft furnishings were thought to harbour the smell of stale food.

Left **Ann Wordsworth** at the dining table

Above **Asparagus rolls**, an 18th-century recipe

The heart of the home

The kitchen ✎

The kitchen would have been at the heart of the Wordsworths' home – a centre of activity, a source of noise, warmth and smells, and a place for the servants and children to eat. But a room like this must have been a tiring environment to work in.

When they were entertaining, Ann would probably have had to roll up her sleeves and help the maid. When they didn't have guests to impress, the family's meals would have been relatively plain.

They would have eaten meat, fish, pies and dairy produce. Vegetables from the garden would have been served boiled, often covered with melted butter. Filled suet puddings and sweet baked puddings were also popular. Apples, rhubarb and gooseberries were eaten raw, added to tarts or made into jams.

Pike and fritters

Ann and her maid would have worked from books such as Elizabeth Raffald's *Experienced English Housekeeper*, where recipes included 'pike boiled with a pudding in the belly', potted char (a local fish), 'calf's head surprise', herb fritters and syllabubs.

Joints and birds would have been roasted on a spit in front of the fire. The spit was turned by a smoke-jack fitted to the chimneybreast, powered by hot air passing over a fan in the flue.

A wood-fired oven, fitted to the right of the range, would have been used for baking bread and cakes. The range is flanked by a charcoal stewing stove (on the left) for making sauces, and a boiling copper (on the right). The tank above the sink would have been filled by buckets, providing water on tap.

Well supplied

The shelves in the arched recess are loaded with pots, pans and jars – the labels show the kind of ingredients available to a comfortably off family like the Wordsworths.

The large centre table is a replica of a traditional design. Its sycamore top can be scrubbed down at the end of the day. A replica dough trough, in which dough was mixed, fermented and left to prove before baking, stands between the windows.

Left Storage jars sealed with chamois leather

Right The maid working in the kitchen

The common parlour ✎

The common parlour was likely to have been used as the equivalent of a modern 'family room' and served as John and Ann's day-to-day dining room. As it was not one of the couple's best rooms, it may have contained more old-fashioned oak furniture of the kind commonly found in mid-18th-century households in the north of England.

The mule chest was made for Thomas Iredale of Cockermouth in 1737, and many of the chairs come from the Lake District. The dresser is laden with the kind of crockery the family would have used on a daily basis: creamware plates and jugs, and pewter dishes and tankards.

Below Dresser in the common parlour

Designed to impress

The drawing room ✎

This grand and imposing room was probably used only when John and Ann were entertaining. After dinner, the ladies would retire here to drink tea and chat. Later, when the men joined them, everyone might have played cards or danced. This is where the Wordsworths would have displayed their most fashionable furniture. When not in use, it would have been fitted with covers, as protection from dust and children.

Done for effect

Paint analysis shows this room was olive green when the Wordsworths moved in. It was the first colour applied to the panelling and carved decoration, installed in the 1740s. The door on the far wall is a fake and is there simply to provide symmetry.

Above Replica Wilton carpet, similar to the one John would have owned at Wordsworth House

Below The drawing room in Odille's day

The furniture – arranged for a social occasion – includes a set of Chippendale armchairs from around 1755 upholstered, under their blue check case covers, in wool damask. The set of early 18th-century walnut chairs with horsehair seats once belonged to poet Robert Southey, and the bureau bookcase from around 1780 was William's in later life.

The advertisement in *The Cumberland Pacquet* listing items for sale after John's death includes 'a large and handsome Wilton carpet'. The replica here was woven to the design of an 18th-century Indian carpet.

The best parlour

Ann might have written letters at her desk, kept her accounts or entertained close friends in this comfortable room overlooking the garden where her children loved to play.

The mahogany kneehole desk is a reproduction of an original from around 1760 made by Lancaster firm Gillows, which produced some of the most fashionable furniture available at the time. Its small size shows it was intended for a lady, who would have been able to lock her papers in the drawers to prevent servants snooping at the contents!

Two fine replica chairs have been fitted with case covers over upholstery of scarlet harrateen, a woollen cloth often chosen for furnishings at the time, which has also been used for the curtains. The wallpaper is a copy of a design from the 1760s. It is block-printed in distemper on small sections of paper – as it would have been then.

Above **The drawing room**

Right **The best parlour**

Musical interlude
We don't know if John and Ann owned an instrument, but if they did it is likely to have been a harpsichord. The one here is a working replica of one made around 1720 by William Smith of London, which may have belonged to Handel. If you are musical, you might like to sit down and play a tune.

Opposite Ann's bedroom

Right *Boy with a Bird's Nest* after Thomas Hudson

Ann Wordsworth's bedroom ✎

The room shown as Ann's bedroom has handsome panelling and a separate closet. It is dominated by a Chippendale-style four-poster bed, hung with fine white linen with a floral sprig pattern. This fabric, based on a design from 1765, is also used for the 'festoon' window curtains. The mid-18th-century oak tripod table is thought to have belonged to Dorothy.

The panelled walls are decorated with embroidered silkwork pictures, an oil portrait – *Boy with a Bird's Nest* in the manner of English artist Thomas Hudson – and an engraving of a Scottish ballad scene, all from the 1760s or 1770s.

Well dressed

The gown on the bed is made of dark red silk taffeta in the 'polonaise' style of the 1770s and would have been worn by a woman of Ann's standing. The closet, decorated with replica 1760s wallpaper, would have been a dressing room. The 1770s chest of drawers belonged to poet Robert Southey.

In the 1930s, doctor's daughter Odille Ellis slept in this room and used the closet as her toy store. Her brother Billy had the room through the connecting doorway, presented as John's bedroom.

Toys and games
Even though their parents were relatively well off, William and his siblings would have had few toys. Most would have been homemade, from wood or cloth. Others might have been bought at fairs and markets.

John Wordsworth's bedroom ✎

John's bed is a replica in the style of Gillows of Lancaster. The footposts – the only visible part of the frame – are African mahogany from sustainable sources; the rest is local oak. The hangings and window curtains are blue harrateen.

Around the bed is a varied collection of furniture, all of high quality and dating from 1720–70, which John might have inherited or bought. The commode corner chair would have housed a chamberpot.

The children's bedroom ✎

It is possible all five children shared this large plain room. From here they would have been able to look out over their favourite playground – the garden and the banks of the River Derwent.

It would probably have been furnished with some of the family's more old-fashioned items. The pine clothes press, table and rocking chair are replicas, made to reflect this.

The early 18th-century oak bed came from Lancashire. It is strung with rope and can't have been particularly comfortable. Wicker cradles were popular at the time, because they were light and airy, and could be burnt easily in case of disease.

Poetic inspiration

The Wordsworth room ✎

This is the one room in the house that isn't presented as it might have been when William was a child, as we wanted it to be a space in which to think about what home means to us today. The settee and longcase clock belonged to him as an adult – and the portrait, by an unknown artist, shows him in middle age. However, the rest of the furnishings are modern.

Love of nature

As his childhood home, this was a place of great happiness and, at times, profound sorrow. His love of family and the natural world that springs from his early years here echoes through his poems.

Although William was just 13 when his father died, five years after his mother, he remembered both his parents with considerable affection.

Of his mother he recalled tenderness, piety and wisdom. From his father he learnt an appreciation of literature – a love for what he later referred to as John's 'golden store' of books.

'Oh! pleasant, pleasant were the days,
The time, when, in our childish plays,
My sister Emmeline and I
Together chased the butterfly!'

To a Butterfly (1801)

In his great autobiographical poem *The Prelude*, which he began in his late 20s and worked on throughout the rest of his life, William reflected on growing up by the River Derwent, which runs past his 'sweet birthplace'. And referring to his sister Dorothy as Emmeline, he wrote in his 1801 poem *To a Butterfly* of their time playing together in the garden here.

If you would like to sit and read, write a poem of your own, or simply reflect for a while, please do so.

Hard times

The death of John and Ann left William, Dorothy and their three brothers 'destitute, and as we might trooping together'. Although, on paper, John looked well off, the property he owned produced only modest rents and much of the rest of his estate consisted of debts owed to him.

The bulk of the money, totalling £4,625 (equivalent to more than £500,000 today), was expenses incurred on behalf of Sir James. However, his employer refused to pay, claiming he had never agreed to cover John's expenses. It was not until Sir James himself died almost 20 years later that his son cleared the debt and the children received their inheritance.

'Was it for this
That one, the fairest of all Rivers, lov'd
To blend his murmurs with my Nurse's song,
And from his alder shades and rocky falls,
And from his fords and shallows, sent a voice
That flow'd along my dreams?'

The Prelude (1805)

Left Portrait of William Wordsworth (artist unknown)

Above *View of Cockermouth* by Samuel Crosthwaite (c.1860)

Right William's porcelain inkwell, 1836

Underground and underwater

The cellars ✎

The cellars face north, helping keep them cool. In the Wordsworths' time, they were divided into three areas. The part closest to the back door was the larder, making it convenient for deliveries and for the kitchen. Raw meat and fish were kept in a meat safe.

Cooked meat, fish, pies and other pastries and dairy products for immediate use were stored on stone benches. Vegetables went underneath.

The middle cellar, now our staff and volunteer tearoom, was used for wine and beer, and accessed from the larder. There was a strong, locked door as well as an inner, timber screen with a second locked door for additional security.

At the east end – now storage – there was a dairy. The Wordsworths kept a cow in a field across the River Derwent and the milk was turned into butter, curds and cheese. The dairy was accessed by a single external door, now blocked up.

Below The cellars, with (left to right) the dairy, the wine and beer cellar, and the larder

By early evening, the water was close to 10 feet deep in some streets and flowing at up to 25mph. More than 500 people were trapped. The emergency services, armed forces, Mountain Rescue, RNLI and Coastguard combed the streets by boat and helicopter, plucking them from windows and roofs.

Scene of devastation

Less than 48 hours later, the water was gone. The team returned to a scene of devastation. Part of the front garden wall and the massive wooden gates were gone. The shop was a wreck, the front courtyard and visitor reception almost impassable with debris.

Inside the house they found a minor miracle – the water had reached only halfway up the joists. The air was heavy with damp, but William's home and its contents had survived. Bolstered by messages of support from around the world, staff and volunteers set to work. They sluiced away tonnes of mud, removed barrow-loads of silt and filled sacks with rubbish.

Weeks of stripping out, building work and refitting followed, and on Saturday, 13 March, Wordsworth House and Garden reopened for its 2010 season, exactly on schedule.

Above At its height, the flood water reached almost to the top of the house steps

Right Flood debris

The great flood

Until Thursday, 19 November 2009, all three parts of the cellar were used for storage. That day the rain gauge at Seathwaite, in nearby Borrowdale, registered more than 300mm in 24 hours – a UK record.

By mid-morning the garden was flooding; by early afternoon, mini geysers were spurting through the cellar wall. Soon, Main Street was a raging torrent and the cellar thigh deep. Staff and volunteers carried John's desk and the Hepplewhite dining chairs upstairs before reluctantly abandoning the house on police instructions.

William's Childhood Playground

William Wordsworth's memories of his early life in Cockermouth were dominated by happy times spent exploring the garden, which was a vital source of produce for the household.

A changing garden

The basic structure of the rear garden, with a smaller walled garden and a raised terrace running parallel to the River Derwent, dates from around the time the house was built in the late 17th century. The steps from the main garden to the terrace were added in the 19th century, probably by Robinson Mitchell.

The National Trust took over the property in 1938, opening it to the public the following year. No major changes were made to the garden until the 1980s, when heritage apple trees and box hedges were added to give it a more 18th-century flavour.

Research in 2003, including a geophysical survey, an archaeological dig, a study of local maps and a comparison with other town gardens of the period, was undertaken to discover how the garden had been altered over the previous 300 years.

John's accounts show that he employed a jobbing gardener and, with so many mouths to feed, it is likely it would have been productive rather than ornamental during the family's time in the house.

In 2004, a central area of lawn was removed and turned into plots for heritage vegetables, while the rest of the garden was replanted with culinary and medicinal herbs and traditional flowering plants, all grown according to modern organic principles.

The flood

The flood of November 2009 laid large areas of the garden to waste. The rushing water wove brightly coloured wool washed out of a local shop around trees and bushes, and left behind other booty including DVDs, chocolate bars, toys and baby clothes, and even a small chest of drawers and a wicker linen basket.

Plants were ripped out by the roots and walls knocked down. The terrace where

Below The 1939 opening party in the garden

William and Dorothy played was decimated – the trees were unsafe and had to be felled and the whole structure had to be rebuilt.

It was a perfect opportunity to make the garden even more authentically Georgian. Vegetable- and flower-beds were realigned to create greater symmetry, and grass paths were replaced with gravel. A summerhouse, cold frames and trellising were erected, a new cut-flower area created and the range of 18th-century plants greatly increased.

Ruined memories
When William and Dorothy visited their childhood playground as young adults, Dorothy recorded their dismay in a letter to her friend Lady Beaumont:

'All was in ruin, the terrace walk buried and choked up with the old privot hedge which had formerly been most beautiful, rose and privot intermingled – the same hedge where the sparrows were used to build their nests.'

Above **Odille's mother and grandmother on the terrace in the 1930s**

Better than ever

The physic beds

The long beds running parallel with the wall borders are physic beds, for plants with medicinal uses. 'Greenup's Pippin' apples – a late 18th-century dual-purpose Lancastrian variety – are underplanted with herbs, including pink and white flowering hyssop, bistort, tansy, feverfew, primrose and cowslip, as well as wild white strawberries and highly scented roses 'Celsiana' and 'Alba Maxima', the white rose of York.

The wall borders

Gravel paths lead between the wall borders and the physic beds. Oak trellising has been constructed with rails six inches apart for fruit fans and espaliers and, in the small walled garden, nine inches apart for climbing plants.

Heritage varieties

The east-facing wall borders (the left-hand wall looking towards the terrace) contain espaliered heritage varieties of pears 'Williams' Bon Chrétien' (1760), 'Louise Bonne of Jersey' and 'Catillac', a culinary pear first recorded in 1665. Growing alongside them are a fig and a fan of Morello cherry.

On the west-facing (right-hand) walls grow 'Hawthornden', a very old Scottish cooking apple, 'Ribston Pippin' and the rare 'Acklam Russet', both Yorkshire apples from the 1700s.

Within low box hedging there are herbs and perennial flowers: day lilies, peonies, asters, Maltese cross, sweet woodruff, red hot pokers, lily of the valley and geraniums. Among the more prominent perennials are angelica, giant scabious and Joe Pye weed.

Under the south-facing terrace walls are plum fans – greengage, claimed to be the oldest plum or gage still in cultivation, and 'Mirabelle de Nancy' with its small yellow fruit. In the autumn, heleniums, asters, rudbeckias and solidago provide colour.

Above An illustration of the main garden

The rose bed

The end bed is planted with two Portugal quinces, whose fruit has a strong floral fragrance and resembles a cross between a pear and a golden apple, and varieties of old-fashioned shrub roses.

These include 'Rosa Mundi', which has large pink, white and crimson blooms and is said to be named after Fair Rosamund, mistress of Henry II; the crimson rose of Lancaster, also known as the apothecary's rose; and 'Quatre Saisons', one of the oldest roses, which has an unusual second flush of flowers in late summer. The bed is edged with aromatic grey-green cat mint.

In spring, tulips mingle with clumps of blue grape hyacinth. Varieties of tulip include the unusual spidery red and yellow 'Acuminata', one of the oldest hybrids; the mildly fragrant scarlet-edged yellow 'Keizerskroon', and the yellow native *Tulipa sylvestris*.

Heritage varieties of tulips, daffodils and crocuses can be found throughout the garden in spring, including William's 'host of golden daffodils' *Narcissus pseudonarcissus lobularis* (Lent lily).

'Trellises may be made of any sort of timber, according to the expense which the owner is willing to bestow… but if any person will go to the expense of oak, it will last much longer.'

Philip Miller,
The Gardeners Dictionary (1768)

Top 'Rosa Mundi'

Above Visitors in the garden

Flowers and food

The cut-flower bed

The end bed nearest the house provides cut-flowers such as asphodel, with grassy foliage and tall spiky yellow flowers; globe thistle, which has clear blue spheres; masterwort, with papery white flowers; Jacob's ladder, whose leaves resemble a series of rungs; the blue bells of campanula, and cone flower, with big purple-red daisy flowers.

The cardoon bed

The triangular bed at the end of the cut-flower bed is dominated by a cardoon, which is similar to a giant artichoke and has spiny silver-grey leaves and large thistle-like purple flower heads. The bed is edged with the dark blue flowering form of hyssop.

The vegetable beds

The central vegetable plots are planted with herbs and flowers mixed with varieties of vegetables available in the 18th century. The gardener rotates these each year to improve the fertility of the soil, just as the Wordsworths' gardener might have done.

Annual flowers such as borage, pot marigold, cornflower and sage are grown as companion plants to the vegetables, to attract bees, assist pollination and distract pests, while crushed egg shells deter slugs.

Golden marjoram, which is a particular favourite with bumble bees, makes a striking edging for the two vegetable plots nearest the house.

Unusual varieties

Among the older and more unusual vegetable varieties cultivated are black Spanish long and round winter radishes, purslane, orach, two forms of beetroot – golden and 'Tonda di Choggia', which has red and white striped flesh – and 'Giant d'Italia' parsley, which resembles celery. The brassica bed has old varieties of cabbages and the cauliflower 'Purple Cape'.

Two of the beds are permanently planted, one with broad-leaved sorrel, horseradish, Good King Henry, salad burnet and Welsh onions, and the other laid out to bushes of gooseberries and red and white currants, interspersed with salad crops.

The last of the beds has runner bean 'Painted Lady' growing up ash poles with two old varieties of sweet pea, 'Matacuna' and 'Painted Lady'. Peas and nasturtiums ramble over hazel sticks woven into a tunnel, alongside asparagus peas and the dwarf French bean 'Lazy Housewife'.

The house's costumed servants collect fruit, vegetables, herbs and edible flowers from the garden to recreate Georgian recipes in the working kitchen. These are also used in cakes, pies, soups and garnishes in the café.

Right The main garden, looking towards the back of the house

Fletch the perchcrow

Fletch the perchcrow, so called because he is too friendly to scare birds, lives in the vegetable beds. We don't know if the Wordsworths had a scarecrow, but they have been in use for thousands of years.

The only perchcrow in the world to have his own blog, Fletch writes about life at Wordsworth House and Garden. Read his musings at fletchthe perchcrow.wordpress.com.

A rosy bower

The terrace

The terrace would have been created as a promenade on which to take exercise and view the river. For William and Dorothy, it was a favourite playground alive with birds and butterflies.

Roses scramble over the walls and weave between the privet bushes: *Rosa arvensis*, which has single creamy flowers and autumnal red hips; the burnet rose (*R. pimpinellifolia*) with masses of creamy flowers followed by blackish hips, and the common sweet briar rose (*R. rubiginosa*) with soft pink flowers and later orange hips.

The henhouse
Records indicate the Wordsworths kept hens. The henhouse is based on woodcuts of rural life by Thomas Bewick (1753–1828). A small flock of Scots Dumpy hens provide eggs for the working kitchen.

Dutch honeysuckles (*Lonicera periclymenum* 'Belgica' and 'Serotina') scent the air, and hellebores, geraniums, Solomon's seal, double meadowsweet and Martagon lilies tumble over the path.

At the west end, an oak Georgian-style summerhouse contains a wind-up audio unit, which plays a selection of William's poetry.

Although there is no evidence of a summerhouse in the Wordsworths' time, an 1839 map shows a small building on this spot, and there were wooden summerhouses on the terrace from the early 19th to the mid-20th centuries.

The small walled garden

The original steps lead from here up to the terrace. In the centre of the lawn are two rare apple trees, 'Red Ladies Finger', a cider apple, and 'Keswick Codlin', a 1790 Lancastrian variety said by Robert Hogg in *The Fruit Manual* (1884) to have been discovered 'growing among a quantity of rubbish behind a wall at Gleaston Castle near Ulverston'.

This area is surrounded by aromatic herbs, including thyme, sweet cicely, rosemary, lemon balm and lovage. The east-facing wall is screened by a hop, which apart from its use in beer, could be harvested in April as an asparagus substitute. The protected sunny lower terrace wall supports a Gagarin blue grape.

On the west-facing wall, roses 'Janet B. Wood' (1768) with creamy white blooms and 'Blush Noisette' (18th century), said to be one of the earliest noisettes, mingle with the small purple bells of *Clematis viticella*, which dates from the 16th century.

In the bed below, the deep crimson bordering on purple flowers of the velvet rose 'Rosa Tuscany' (pre-1596) are offset by the silvery leaves of southernwood and wormwood and the feathery foliage of bronze fennel.

The cut-flower bed

The small cut-flower bed has been planted with choice 18th-century flowers including asters, campanulas, phloxes, thalictrums and rudbeckias to grace the best rooms in the house. Growing by the wall is the little-known 16th-century small black bullace, a relative of the plum, with a bitter fruit that can be used in jams.

Wordsworth House and Garden Today

Around 80 volunteers donate their time and skills to help make William and Dorothy Wordsworth's childhood home the vibrant, special place it is today. They welcome and chat to visitors, give guided tours and assist in the garden, café and shop.

If you have enjoyed your visit to Wordsworth House and Garden, and have a few hours to spare, on a regular or occasional basis, why not talk to us about joining our team of volunteers?

Or if you are looking for a unique venue for a wedding or other family celebration, or even a business event, ask about hiring the house and garden that inspired one of our greatest poets.

'Behold, within the leafy shade,
Those bright blue eggs together laid!
On me the chance-discovered sight
Gleamed like a vision of delight.
I started – seeming to espy
The home and sheltered bed,
The Sparrow's dwelling, which, hard by
My father's house, in wet or dry
My sister Emmeline and I
Together visited.'

The Sparrow's Nest (1801)

Below Volunteers in the garden